GREAT LITTLE BOOK OF
Story Book
ACTIVITIES

D0669498

**Published by Playmore Inc., Publishers
and Waldman Publishing Corp.,
New York, New York**

Finish Me

Use the squares below to finish the other half of Humpty Dumpty.

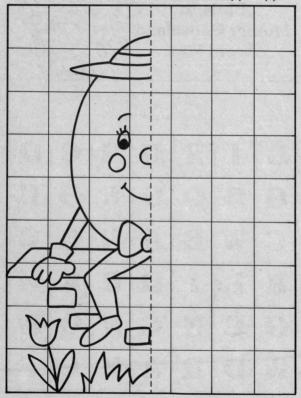

Birds In Mother Gooseland Word Find

Find the words in the word list by looking up,
down, diagonally and across.
Circle the words you find.

B	I	R	D	H	C	D
G	O	O	S	E	O	U
C	W	B	A	N	C	C
R	L	I	D	B	K	K
O	C	N	C	R	O	W
W	D	R	A	K	E	F

Halfway Drawing Fun

Use the dotted lines and the squares below
to draw Little Boy's Blue frolicking cow!

Mittens for the Kittens

Color the mittens with circles blue.
Color the mittens with stars green.
Color the mittens with hearts red.

Find the Difference

These **2** pictures look exactly alike, but look again.
Can you find **4** places where they are different?

I Can Count

Help Little Boy Blue count
all the sheep in
the meadow!

Find and Color

Find Yankee Doodle's horse and color him brown!

Find the Difference

These **2** pictures look exactly alike, but look again.
Can you find **3** places where they are different?

Mother Goose's Food Word Find

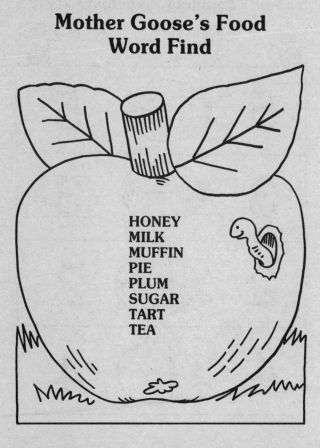

HONEY
MILK
MUFFIN
PIE
PLUM
SUGAR
TART
TEA

Ladybug, Ladybug!

Put the right number of dots on each
lady bug. Now write the number.

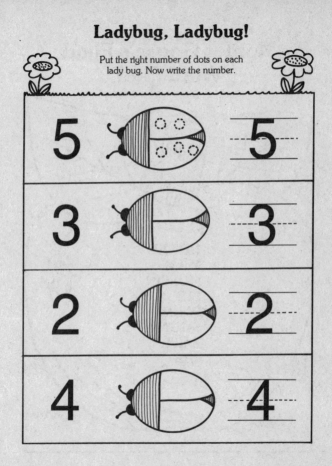

Color by Number

The 3 Little Kittens

1-Green   2-Blue   3-Yellow   4-Grey
5-Red   6-Orange   7-White

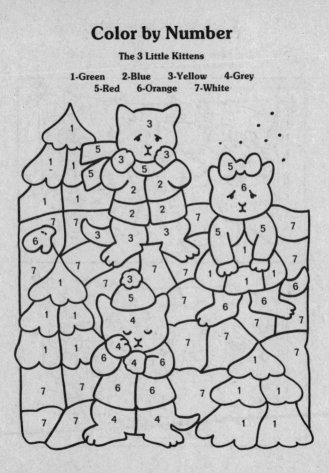

Find the Differences

These **2** pictures look alike, but look again! Can you find **6** places where they are different?

Find and Color

3 Little Kittens have lost **5** mittens.
Color the ones you find.

Scrambled Pigs

How many little pigs
can you find?

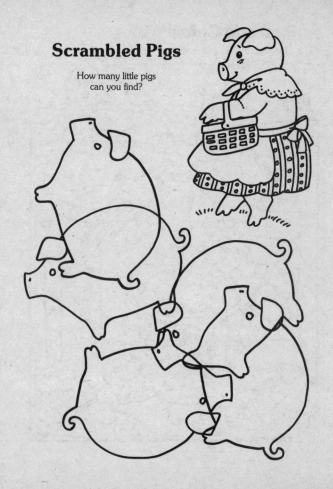

Find and Color

Find **2** of Bo-Peep's sheep and color them pink!

Mother Goose's Animal Word Find

Find the words in the word list by looking up,
down, diagonally and across.
Circle the words you find.

A	D	F	I	S	H	C
H	O	R	S	E	O	F
D	G	E	G	M	G	B
C	O	W	P	I	G	A
L	I	O	N	C	A	T
H	R	A	T	E	I	K

Word Balloon

What did Pussy Cat say?

Write the first letter of each
picture in the balloon to
find the answer.

Answer: Mew

Color by Number

Punch and Judy

1-Pink **2-Green** **3-Blue** **4-Yellow** **5-Red**
6-White **7-Orange** **8-Purple**

Mountain Maze

OUT

IN

Help Huck climb to the top of this mountain.

Birds in
Mother Gooseland
Word Find

BIRD
COCK
CROW
DRAKE
DUCK
GOOSE
HEN
OWL
ROBIN

A Circus Visitor

Follow the dots and find what Huck saw when the circus came to town.

Hidden Picture—4

A bird is hiding from Huck in the space between the clouds. Can you find the bird . . . and also three other animals hidden in this picture?

Black Hen's Good Food Word Find

Find the words in the word list by looking up,
down, diagonally and across.
Circle the words you find.

C	H	E	R	R	Y	C
A	P	P	L	E	B	O
K	B	L	O	G	U	O
E	E	N	M	G	N	K
B	E	A	N	S	S	Y
P	F	B	R	E	A	D

Alphabet Oops!

Huck is learning the letters of the alphabet. But he forgot 7 of them.
Find the missing letters and write them in the boxes.

Scrambled Ducks

How many ducks did Huck see on the river?

Mississippi Bird Count

As Huck and Jim floated down the Mississippi River, they saw migrating birds. How many birds are there?

Black Hen's Good Food
Word Find

APPLE BEANS BREAD BEEF BUNS CAKE CHERRY COOKY EGGS

Rowboat Maze

IN

OUT

Help Huck across the Mississippi in his rowboat.

Mother Goose's Animal Word Find

BAT	FISH	MICE
CAT	HOG	PIG
COW	HORSE	RAT
DOG	LION	

Huck's Runaway Word Search

S	E	O	H	S	L
S	O	A	P	L	E
H	L	C	E	N	F
I	A	W	K	B	I
R	O	P	E	S	N
T	E	P	I	P	K

PIPE
SHOES
SHIRT
TOWEL
SOCKS
SOAP
ROPE
KNIFE

When Huck ran away from home, he carried many things in his bag. Those things are in the word list. Find them in the puzzle by looking up and down, forward and backward, and diagonally. Circle the words you find.

Huck's Tools

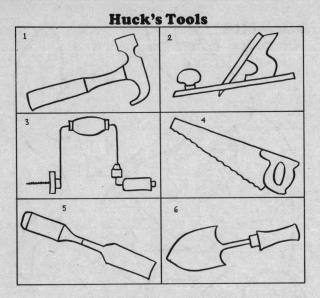

Huck uses 5 of these tools when he works with wood.
Can you find the one that would not be used with wood?

Scrambled Pictures

Can you find 5 animals that Huck saw in the woods?

Letter Fun

Jumping Joan has **OA** in her name. Can you write other words with **OA** in them?

Write the first letter of each picture in the box beneath it to spell out these words.

| | O | A | |

A Lost Pipe

Huck lost his pipe somewhere on this steamboat.
Can you find it?
Then color the picture.

Girls' Names
in Mother Goose
Word Find

Find the words in the word list by looking up,
down, diagonally and across.
Circle the words you find.

M	A	H	S	U	E	I
A	N	N	A	D	K	J
R	P	O	L	L	Y	E
Y	B	J	L	O	E	N
G	F	M	Y	C	L	N
B	E	T	T	Y	P	Y

Word Balloon

Who ate the malt in Jack's house?

1 ___ 2 ___ 3 ___

Write the first letter of
each picture in the balloon
to find the answer.

Shadow Match

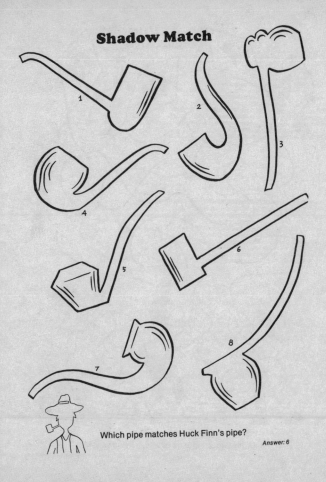

Which pipe matches Huck Finn's pipe?

Answer: 6

Tangled Kites

Trace the kite string and see who is flying each kite.

Finish Me!

Use the squares below to finish the other half of Mother Goose.

Find the Difference

These **2** pictures look exactly alike, but look again.
Can you find **5** places where they are different?

Halfway Drawing Fun

Use the dotted lines and the squares below to
draw Mary's little lamb who followed
her to school.

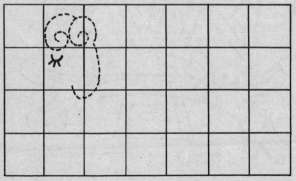

Huck heard this owl hoot at midnight. Find your way through this owl maze.

Tommy Tucker's Clothes
Word Find

COAT
HAT
GLOVES
PANTS
SCARF
SHIRT
SHOES
SOCKS
VEST

**Girls' Names
in Mother Goose
Word Find**

ANNA
BETTY
JENNY
MARY
POLLY
SALLY
SUE

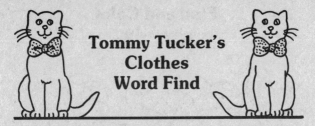

Tommy Tucker's Clothes Word Find

Find the words in the word list by looking up,
down, diagonally and across.
Circle the words you find.

S	H	S	C	A	R	F
H	G	L	O	V	E	S
I	J	L	A	E	I	H
R	H	A	T	S	N	O
T	P	A	N	T	S	E
K	M	S	O	C	K	S

Find and Color

Help Bo-Peep find **5** lost sheep.
Color the ones you find.

Bean Patch Maze

Red Riding Hood must go through the bean patch to get to the path in the woods.

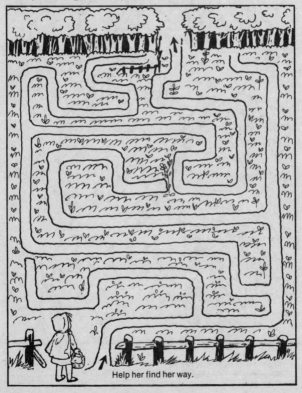

Help her find her way.

Can you find these hidden pictures: bone, mitten, ant, pie, sock, horn, turtle, mouse, apple, elephant, moon, bat, safety pin, fish, drum, arrow, whale?

Which path will lead Jack to the castle?

SURPRISE

What did Jack say to his mother when he got home?

Find the answer by crossing out all the letters that appear in the diagram 4 times.

J	P	V	L	O	F	D
D	O	K		J	P	M
O	V	T	P	H	D	E
F	R	J		M	A	V
G	I	F	C	D	J	B
V	E	P	A	N	F	S

DRAWING LESSON

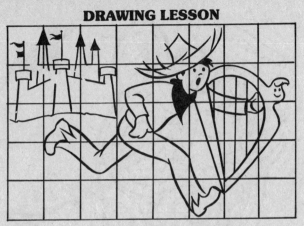

Draw Jack and his harp in the squares below.

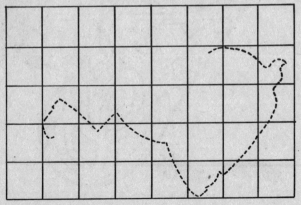

Help Jack follow the footstep on his way to the castle.

Down the Hole

Alice fell down the rabbit hole, drifting slowly past cupboards and pictures.

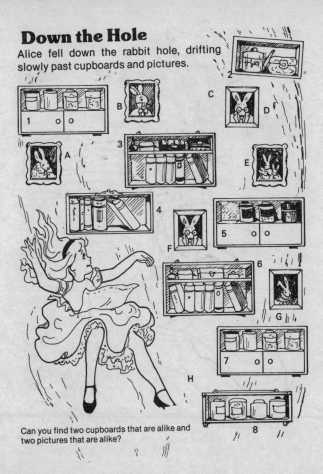

Can you find two cupboards that are alike and two pictures that are alike?

Help Jack escape to the beanstalk.

Flamingo Mallet

Alice found the Flamingo a difficult mallet for playing croquet.

How many 3- and 4-letter words can you make from the letters in **FLAMINGO?**

_____ _____ _____ _____

_____ _____ _____ _____

_____ _____ _____ _____

_____ _____ _____ _____

_____ _____ _____ _____

_____ _____ _____ _____

An A-MAZE-ing Garden

Help Alice find her way through the garden to the croquet ground.

Just a Pack of Cards?

The cards flew up at Alice.

At first, she thought they were all different,
but then she saw two exactly alike.
Find them.

Pool of Tears

After Alice woke the crabs, she met another creature swimming in the water. Who was it?

1-pink   2-gray   3-blue   4-white   5-yellow

White Rabbit's Tidy Room

Alice went to the White Rabbit's room to look for his fan. In the room she saw many things beginning with the letter "F".

How many can you find?

Be A-Mazed

Help Alice find her way to the mushroom.

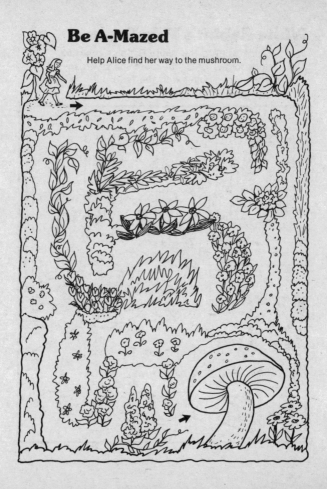

Smoke Maze
Help Alice find her way to the Duchess.

Tea Table

When Alice looked at the table set for tea she saw many plates, cups, saucers, and spoons. But only two of the plates matched, and only two cups and saucers matched, and only two spoons matched.

Can you find these matches?

Answers: plates 1 and 7, cups and saucers G and H, and spoons 13 and 16

Twins

Red Riding Hood passes neighbor's pig farm.

His pigs look alike, but only 2 are twins. Can you find them?

Through the Woods

Help Red Riding Hood find her way to Grandmother's house.

"What **BIG TEETH** you have!" said Red Riding Hood.

wolf answered, "The better

to ___ ___ ___   ___ ___ ___!"

Use the picture clues to fill in the words across. Then, the 2 words formed going down in the heavy lines will finish the sentence.

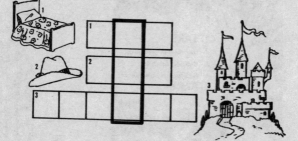

Dark Woods

Red Riding Hood has to **TAKE** the path through the dark **PART** of the woods.

Can you change the word **TAKE** to the word **PART** in 4 moves? Change only one letter each time. Each change will fit a clue.

1. **TAKE**
2. One food in her basket
3. Caution, attention
4. A horse-drawn vehicle
5. **PART**

1. TAKE
2. _____
3. _____
4. _____
5. PART

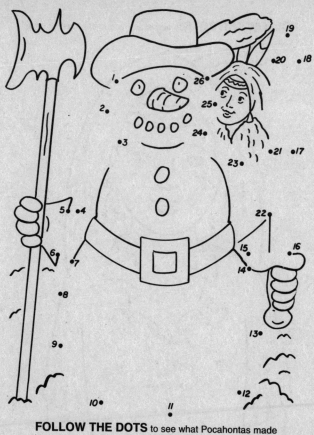

FOLLOW THE DOTS to see what Pocahontas made in the winter!

FOLLOW THE DOTS to see what Pocahontas liked to wear!

Help Jack get out of the castle.

Can you help Jack get free of the giant?

Color by Number

Oh! Oh! Who will Red Riding Hood meet next?

1-green   2-yellow   3-blue   4-gray   5-red

Path Talk

"Where are you going?" asked the wolf.

"To Grandmother's," said Red Riding Hood.

"Where does she live?" asked the wolf, pretending to be friendly.

Red Riding Hood answered, "Down the
1 _ _ _ _, past the 2 _ _ _ _, in a
3 _ _ _ _ _ under three 4 _ _ _ trees
by a thorny 5 _ _ _ _ _."

Unscramble the words and fill in the blanks.

1. THAP   2. LIML   3. SOEHU

4. OKA   5. GHEED

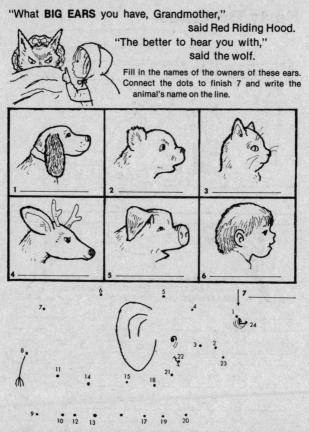

"What **BIG EARS** you have, Grandmother,"
said Red Riding Hood.
"The better to hear you with,"
said the wolf.

Fill in the names of the owners of these ears. Connect the dots to finish 7 and write the animal's name on the line.

1 _____ 2 _____ 3 _____

4 _____ 5 _____ 6 _____

7 _____

Early Breakfast

Would you like to take a basket to your grandmother?

How many 3- and 4-letter words can you find in the word BREAKFAST? Little Red Riding Hood found 40 words. Can you find them too?

_____   _____   _____   _____
_____   _____   _____   _____
_____   _____   _____   _____
_____   _____   _____   _____
_____   _____   _____   _____
_____   _____   _____   _____
_____   _____   _____   _____
_____   _____   _____   _____

Hidden Pictures

Red Riding Hood waves to her uncle, the woodcutter, as she passes him in the woods.

But where is his ax? It's hidden in the picture, along with 3 birds and 3 rabbits. Can you find them?

Red Riding Hood said, "What _ _ _ _
_ _ _ _ _ you have!"

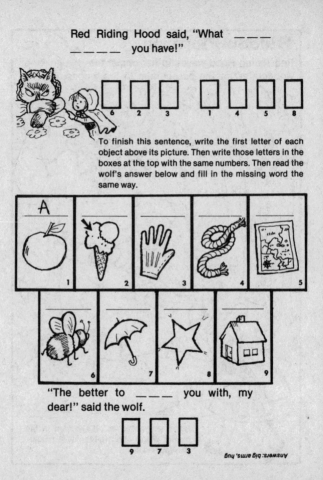

To finish this sentence, write the first letter of each object above its picture. Then write those letters in the boxes at the top with the same numbers. Then read the wolf's answer below and fill in the missing word the same way.

"The better to _ _ _ you with, my dear!" said the wolf.

Answers: big arms, hug

How Many?

Red Riding Hood sees birds on each branch of a tree.

Write the number of birds in the box at the end of each branch. Add up the numbers and write the answer in the square under the tree.

The Path Home

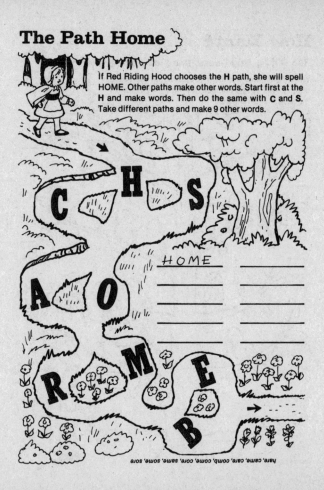

If Red Riding Hood chooses the **H** path, she will spell HOME. Other paths make other words. Start first at the **H** and make words. Then do the same with **C** and **S**. Take different paths and make 9 other words.

HOME _____ _____

_____ _____ _____

_____ _____ _____

_____ _____ _____

hare, came, care, comb, come, core, same, some, sore

Follow the Dots

Follow the dots and see who is
chasing Red Riding Hood.

Find a Pair

Help little Red Riding Hood find the matching socks.

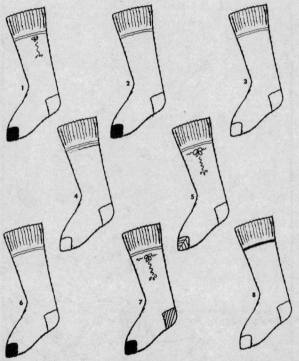

Answers: 2 and 6

Cozy Cupboard

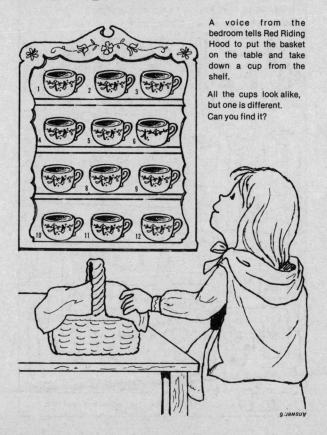

A voice from the bedroom tells Red Riding Hood to put the basket on the table and take down a cup from the shelf.

All the cups look alike, but one is different. Can you find it?

Forest Flowers Maze

While little Red Riding Hood was picking flowers, she wandered off the path.

PATH   Help her find her way back to it.

Scrambled Closet

Unscramble the names of the clothes in little Red Riding Hood's closet.

SRESD

_ _ _ _ _

HESOS

_ _ _ _ _

GKOTSSCIN

_ _ _ _ _ _ _ _ _

RAPON

_ _ _ _ _

Garden Maze

Before breakfast, Red Riding Hood must get water at the well.

Help her find the way.

Flowers

The wolf told little Red Riding Hood to pick some flowers.

What kind of flowers did she see?

Unscramble the name of each flower and write it below the picture. Color the flowers by following the clues:) = yellow, ■ = purple, ✿ = red, • = orange. Color all the leaves green.

1. YLIL
_ _ _ _

2. LOVITE
_ _ _ _ _ _

3. PYOPP
_ _ _ _ _

4. SIADY
_ _ _ _ _

5. VERLOC
_ _ _ _ _ _

6. CUTUBPRET
_ _ _ _ _ _ _ _ _

Color by Number

Red Riding Hood will see a little animal in
the woods. Who is that animal?

1-   2-yellow   3-green   4-black   5-brown

Tricky Thirteen!

Pinocchio has found 8 ways for the numbers on this puzzle to add up to 13. Look across, down, and diagonally to find these ways. Pinocchio has circled one way — 4 + 7 + 2. Find the other 7 ways and circle them.

Color by Number

Help Pinocchio find his favorite pet.

1-blue 2-green 3-orange 4-yellow 5-pink 6-white

Hidden Kites

Like all kids, Pinocchio loves to fly kites. But there's more than just the one kite Pinocchio is flying in this picture — there are 16 kites all together. Can you find all 16 hidden kites?

Pinocchio's Word Game

The words in each column are words all by themselves. But if you put two words together, they form one new word. That kind of word is called a **compound** word. Draw a line from each word in the first column to a word in the second column and make a new compound word.

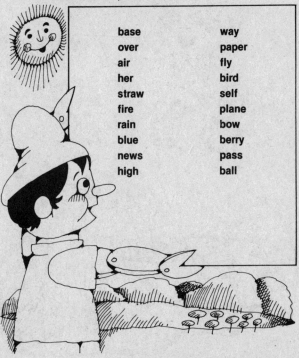

base	way
over	paper
air	fly
her	bird
straw	self
fire	plane
rain	bow
blue	berry
news	pass
high	ball

School Days!

Pinocchio had a habit of wandering off the path whenever he was on the way to school. Show him the right path from Geppetto's house to the schoolhouse.

Sweet Stuff

Goldilocks loves all kinds of candy for dessert. Those candies are in the word list below. Find the words in the word list by looking across, down, diagonally, forwards, and backwards. Circle the words you find.

CANDY CANE
CHOCOLATE
FUDGE
GUMDROP
LICORICE
LOLLIPOP
SOURBALL
TAFFY

```
L S C H O C O L A T E
O B I U C H G E G U Z
L N E G D U F U H O V
L S L I M P I P E O I
I C M D V N C N I V E
P B R V U O A I F N C
O O I C D C F L V W I
P D C U Y F F A T O R
L V O D L I C O L C O
V I N U O U I C U O C
I A O V C E L F L D I
C I D S O U R B A L L
```

Hidden Fruits

Goldilocks is in a magical fruit forest where 8 kinds of fruit are hidden. Help her find them.

Apple Tree Maze

Help Goldilocks climb the apple tree to get to the ripe, delicious apples.

Where Will Pinocchio Go?

Pinocchio has just escaped from Stromboli. Trace the tangled lines to help him get back to Geppetto and give the other puppets to Stromboli.

A Surprise At Sea

Follow the dots and see who Pinocchio meets out at sea.

Hidden Hats

Ten hats just like the one Pinocchio is wearing are hidden in this forest on Pleasure Island. Can you find all 10?

"Help Me Get Home!" Maze

Pinocchio wants more than anything else to get home to Geppetto. Help him find his way out of this maze.

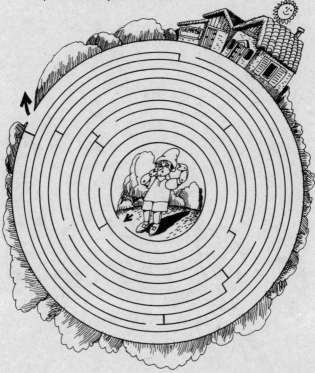

FEATHER JUMBLE

Pocahontas needs a new feather. How many feathers
are in the jumble below?

POCAHONTAS LETTER P GAME

Which items in the picture begin with the letter P?
Color the whole picture.

SHADOW FUN

Which shadow matches the picture of Pocahontas
in her English gown?

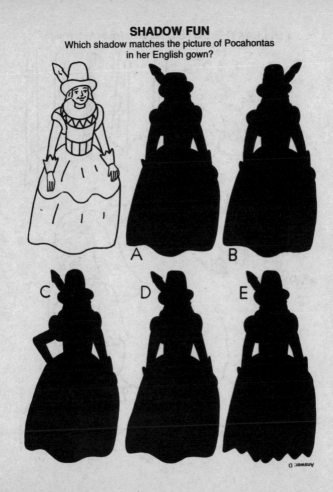

A

B

C

D

E

Answer: D

FOLLOW THE DOTS to see who chased Pocahontas.

FOLLOW THE DOTS to see who Pocahontas could always outrun.

DRAWING FUN

Can you finish the other half of Hercules. The dotted lines will help you get started.

COLOR BY NUMBER—HERCULES

1: Red	4: Yellow	7: Brown
2: Blue	5: Orange	8: Black
3: Green	6: Purple	9: Pink

A Strange Garden!

Goldilocks sees some strange things in the Three Bears' garden. Find 7 things wrong with this picture.

A Long Walk Rebus

Where did Goldilocks go on her long walk?

Solve the rebus by adding or subtracting the letters according to the signs.

Answer: forest

Peek at "P"

Goldilocks peeks into the Three Bears' living room and sees 10 things that begin with the letter "P". Can you find all 10?

Poor Goldilocks is lost in the deep forest. But finally, she sees a little house beyond the trees. Help her find her way to the little house.

FOLLOW THE DOTS to see the dress pattern
Pocahontas used.

IN PRISON

Quick! Help Hercules free his friend Theseus.

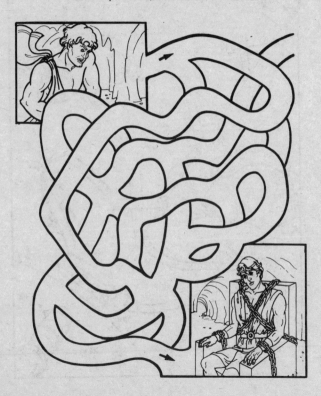

FOLLOW THE DOTS

See if you can find Hercules's favorite weapon!

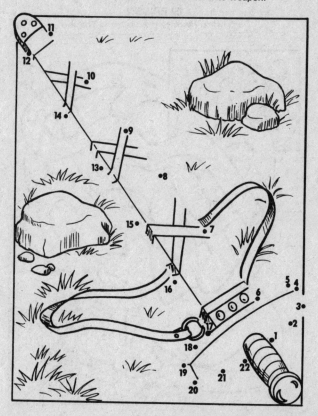

FOLLOW THE DOTS

Can you find the special treasure Hercules was seeking?

WHO GETS THE APPLES?

Only 1 path leads to the golden apples.
Who gets there, Hercules or Atlas?

SHADOW MATCH

Which Hercules exactly matches the shadow?

WORD FIND

Look in up, down, across and even backwards in the grid below to find the names of the characters below. In the small square write the number of times you find their names.

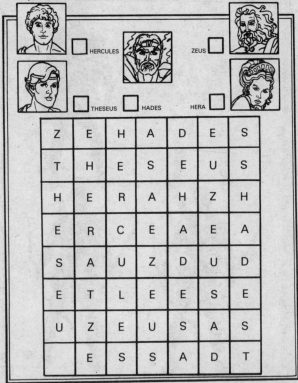

HERCULES

ZEUS

THESEUS

HADES

HERA

Z	E	H	A	D	E	S
T	H	E	S	E	U	S
H	E	R	A	H	Z	H
E	R	C	E	A	E	A
S	A	U	Z	D	U	D
E	T	L	E	E	S	E
U	Z	E	U	S	A	S
	E	S	S	A	D	T

MOUNTAIN MAZE

Help Theseus reach his friend Hercules as they explore together.

FOLLOW THE DOTS to find what Hercules had to capture.

ARROW MAZE

Hercules shot 2 arrows. Starting from the arrows find
which birds and how many of them Hercules hit.

LET'S MEET

Hercules and Theseus are meeting at the tree stump to practice their archery. Can you find the path for both of them?

HIDDEN PICTURE

Can you find the lion hiding from Hercules in the picture below?

I CAN FIND IT!

Help Hercules reach the oracle at Delphi.

FOLLOW THE DOTS to see where Hercules kept his arrows.

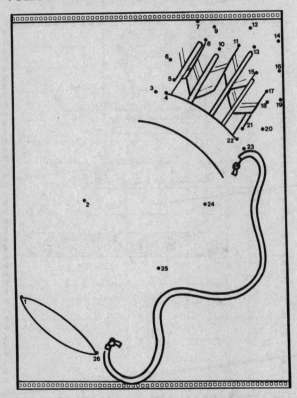

WORD FUN

Use the first letter of the small pictures below in the squares
beneath them to complete the sentence.

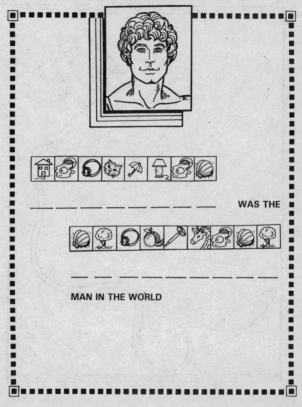

_ _ _ _ _ _ _ _   **WAS THE**

_ _ _ _ _ _ _ _ _

MAN IN THE WORLD

HIDDEN PICTURE

Hercules must hunt a magic deer. Can you help him?

FOLLOW THE DOTS

What did Hercules love to practice?

Which Word?

Poor Pinocchio! He's come across some words that are really puzzling him because they sound alike but are spelled differently and have different meanings. These words are called **homonyms**. Draw lines to connect the homonyms in the two trees.

so	read
bear	son
red	blew
seen	lone
rain	rein
blue	sew
loan	bare
sun	scene

Puppet Materials

Pinocchio is a puppet that Geppetto made out of wood. But puppets can be made from other materials too. Those materials are in the word list below. Find those words in the puzzle by looking across, down, backwards, forwards, and diagonally. Circle the words you find.

WOOD
ROCK
METAL
STONE
CLAY
PLASTER
MUD
CLOTH
PAPER
PLASTIC

```
A I R E P A P F
W O O D M B H N
U H C S M U C I
I O K D E D H R
C O D S T O N E
C L A Y A Z I T
B U O Z L E U S
V I E T U O V A
D U M I H B W L
O C I T S A L P
```

Catching Cleo

Pinocchio is trying to get to Cleo's bowl. But the line to her bowl is tangled with the lines to three other fishbowls. Trace the correct line from Pinocchio to Cleo.

Forgetful Pinocchio!

When it was time to leave school, Pinocchio forgot the way to Geppetto's house. Help him find the way.

Ice Cream Cone Twins

"What a great place Pleasure Island is!" said Pinocchio.
"There are ice cream cones growing out of the ground!" Help
Pinocchio find the twin cones.

Lucky 13

Goldilocks' lucky number is 13. She has found 9 ways that the numbers on this puzzle add up to 13, but she has circled only one way — 8 + 2 + 3. Find the other 8 ways by looking across, down, and diagonally, and circle them too.

10	2	5	8
2	12	6	2
1	7	2	3
9	12	10	4

Scrambled Names

Goldilocks has taken 3 pictures with her camera. Unscramble the name that goes with each picture and draw a line to that picture.

1. AYBB EARB

2. APPA ERBA

3. AMAM RBAE

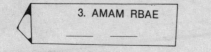

_____

A Strange Forest!

Pinocchio is looking for Geppetto in this strange forest. Can you find **7** things wrong in this forest?

Across-and-Down Crossword

Help Goldilocks solve this crossword puzzle. All the words read the same across and down.

1. Take with force
2. What you do on a horse
3. Increases
4. The greatest

5. Snare
6. Running contest
7. Pretends
8. Nuisance

Apple Tangle

Each of Pinocchio's apples grew on a different tree.
Trace the tangled lines to see where each came from.

Strange Friends!

Pinocchio and his friends look rather strange in this picture.
Can you find **9** things wrong in the picture?

Ten Tally

Who did Goldilocks meet in the deep forest?

To find the answer, solve the number problems in each box. For each box whose answer is 10, circle the letter in that box. If the answer is not 10, leave the letter alone. All the circled letters will spell out the answer to the question.

7+3=	11−3=	9+1=	6+6=	4+6=	10+1=	6+7=
T	O	H	Z	E	S	L

2+8=	4+8=	1+9=	10+0=	12−2=	5+6=	5+5=
T	C	H	R	E	M	E

8+4=	6+4=	0+10=	15−6=	3+7=	8+2=	13−3=
D	B	E	O	A	R	S

Pinocchio's Animal Friends

Pinocchio met many animals in his travels. These animals are in the word list below. Find those words in the puzzle by looking across, down, backwards, forwards, and diagonally. Circle the words you find.

GOLDFISH
CRICKET
DONKEY
WHALE
FOX
DOVE
CAT

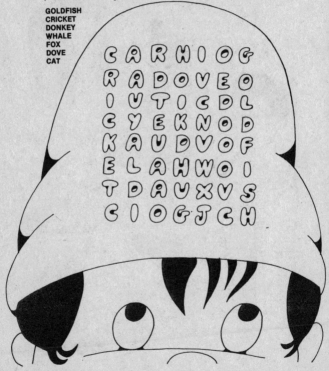

```
C A R H I O G
R A D O V E O
I U T I C D L
C Y E K N O D
K A U D V O F
E L A H W O I
T D A U X V S
C I O G J C H
```

Find the Twins

Help Pinocchio find the twin hats. There are 3 pairs of twins.

Across and Down Crossword

Goldilocks' crossword puzzle reads the same across and down.
Use the clues to fill in the words.

1. A fastener for clothing
2. What you call yourself
3. The word at the end of a prayer
4. Writing tools

The Magical 5 Forest

In the Magical 5 Forest, 5's are hidden everywhere.
How many can you find?

Two Apples a Day!

If an apple a day keeps the doctor away, perhaps 2 apples a day will keep lies away from Pinocchio. Can you find 2 apples that look exactly alike?

Color by Number

Pinocchio's friend is waiting patiently for him to come home.

1-orange   2-red   3-purple   4-light blue   5-pink   6-yellow

A Starry Night

Pinocchio sees many stars in the sky. But he also see stars in some strange places too. Help Pinocchio count all the stars.

Pinocchio's Puzzle

Solve Pinocchio's puzzle using the clues below. The words read the same across and down.

1. Auto
2. Drink made with lemon
3. Color of blood

4. Lie
5. Frozen water
6. Plead

Pinocchio's Favorite Fruit

Follow the dots and see what fruit Pinocchio can't wait to eat!

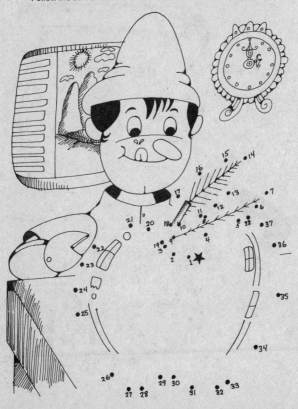

Hidden Words in GEPPETTO

Use the letters in the name GEPPETTO to make 3-letter words. Pinocchio found 12 three-letter words. Can you find those 12 . . . or more?

GEPPETTO

Whale Maze

While looking for Geppetto, Pinocchio was swallowed by a whale.
Help Pinocchio find his way out of the whale.

A Forest Creature

Follow the dots and see who Pinocchio met in the forest.

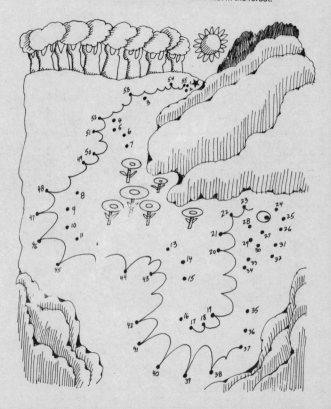

"Come to Me, Son!"

Help Pinocchio get to Geppetto without winding up on Pleasure Island or in the jaws of Monstro the Whale.

A Nesting Place!

Pinocchio told a lie — and look at his nose! These birds built a nest on it. But only two of these birds are from the same family. Look at the birds carefully and decide which two they are.

Answer: 2 and 5

Hidden P's

Sixteen P's are hidden in Pinocchio's garden. Can you find all 16?

A Real Boy!

Geppetto was very happy when Pinocchio finally became a real boy. Find the correct path from Geppetto to the *real* — not the puppet — Pinocchio.

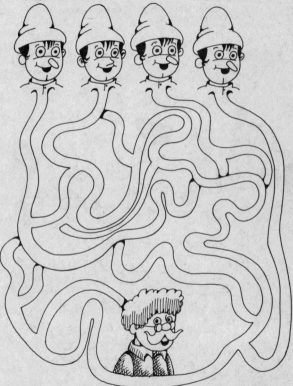

Forwards and Backwards Crossword

Help Goldilocks solve this crossword puzzle. All the words read the same forwards and backwards or up and down.

ACROSS

2. Short for Mother
6. A female sheep
7. Short for Sister
8. A small dog

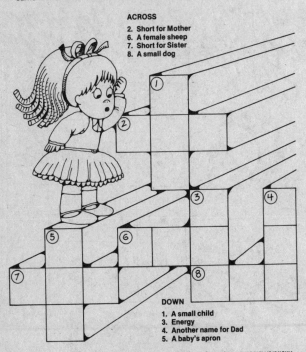

DOWN

1. A small child
3. Energy
4. Another name for Dad
5. A baby's apron

Tricky 21

Goldilocks found 11 ways for the numbers in this puzzle to add up to 21. She has circled one way — 10 + 10 + 1. Find the other 10 ways by looking across, down, and diagonally. Circle the ways you find.

10	8	2	1
6	14	10	9
5	10	6	11
10	8	3	1

Homonym Hunt

Homonyms are words that sound the same, but are spelled differently and have different meanings. Help Goldilocks match the homonyms in the two columns by drawing a line to connect each pair.

DEW	HEAL
KNEW	BEET
SIZE	BRAKE
BEAT	SIGHS
HEEL	ONE
BREAK	DUE
DEER	ATE
WON	NEW
EIGHT	TOO
TWO	DEAR

To the Grocer Maze

Goldilocks has offered to do Mama Bear's shopping.
Help her find her way to the grocery store.

IN THE SWIM!

Color each dotted area purple to see how many fish are swimming with Pocahontas. Color all the other areas blue.

DESIGN A DRESS

Pocahontas was a beautiful bride.
Can you design her wedding dress?

FOLLOW THE DOTS to see the state Pocahontas lived in.

CIRCLE FUN!
How many circles can you find in this picture of
Pocahontas and John Rolfe?

Answer: 12

NATIVE CODE

Pocahontas was baptized and took an English name.
Using the code, write her new name.
Now write your name and then write it in code.

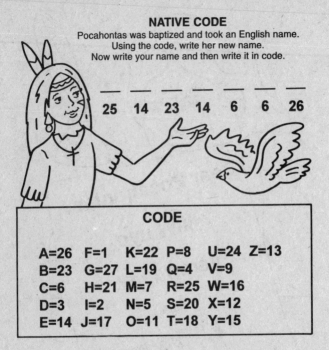

_ _ _ _ _ _ _
25 14 23 14 6 6 26

CODE

A=26   F=1   K=22   P=8   U=24   Z=13
B=23   G=27   L=19   Q=4   V=9
C=6   H=21   M=7   R=25   W=16
D=3   I=2   N=5   S=20   X=12
E=14   J=17   O=11   T=18   Y=15

YOUR NAME

YOUR NAME IN CODE

NOTE SCRAMBLE
John Rolfe fell in love with Pocahontas. Unscramble the letters to see what his note says.

Answer: Will you marry me?

STAR COUNT
Color the areas with dots black to see how many
stars Pocahontas sees.

POCAHONTAS WORD GAME

Use the letters from the words in the center square to spell the other pictures.

POCAHONTAS

LONDON MATCH
Pocahontas loved London when she visited it. Which of each group of 3 matches most closely the picture in the first box.

MOCCASIN JUMBLE

Pocahontas wore moccasins to protect her feet. How many can you find in the jumble below?

FISH TANGLE

Which rope should Pocahontas pull on to catch the fish?

FOLLOW THE DOTS to see how Pocahontas was captured.

CANDLE MATCH

Which two candles exactly match the one Pocahontas is holding?

```
ZTABCZHDEFZEPOCAHONTASZOJOHNSMI
THZNPOWHATANZEJAMESTOWNZWZHFGH
IJKZOGENGLANDZPABCZLNATIVEAMERIC
ANZAABCZYAFHKISVBZSSWASEYZMZOZS
KINGJAMESZTABCDZLAFGOPQRTKLZYAB
```

_ _ _ _ _ _ _ _ _

_ _ _ _ _ _ _ _ _ _

Z CODE

Circle every letter that follows the letter Z and write those letters in
order to find out what the name Pocahontas means.